Presented to

_____

From

_____

On This Date

_____

Desserts

WANDA E. BRUNSTETTER'S
Amish Friends Cookbook

BARBOUR
PUBLISHING

Cover Credit: Judd Pilossof / FoodPix / Getty Images
Photographs on pages 52, 74, 94, 116, 136 © Doyle Yoder, www.dypinc.com
Photography on pages 17, 20, 45, 57, 60, 71, 85, 96, 103, 133, 141, 146 by Jim Celuch, Celuch Creative Imaging.
Photographed desserts prepared by Ashley Casteel, Jessie Fioritto, Rebecca Germany, Krista Komaromy, Emily Morelli, Samantha Phillips, Ashley Schrock, Annie Tipton, Louise Worsham, and Terra Zoladz.

Published by Barbour Publishing, Inc., P.O. Box 719, Uhrichsville, Ohio 44683, www.barbourbooks.com

Our mission is to publish and distribute inspirational products offering exceptional value and biblical encouragement to the masses.

Member of the
Evangelical Christian
Publishers Association

Printed in China.

Contents

A Brief History of the Amish and Mennonites

The Amish and Mennonites are direct descendants of the Anabaptists, a group that emerged from the Reformation in Switzerland in 1525 and developed separately in Holland a few years later. Most Anabaptists eventually became identified as Mennonites, after a prominent Dutch leader, Menno Simons. The word *Amish* comes from Jacob Ammann, an influential leader who in 1963 led a group that separated from the Mennonite churches.

Driven by persecution from their homes in Switzerland and Germany, hundreds of Mennonites began to immigrate to North America, and in the 1700s, the Amish sought homes in North America, too. They were welcomed in Pennsylvania by William Penn and first settled there by the mid-nineteenth century. Some moved to Ohio, Indiana, Iowa, and other parts of the country. Both the Amish and Mennonites believe in the authority of the scriptures, and their willingness to stand apart from the rest of the world shows through their simple, plain way of living.

Wunderbaar Gut (Wonderful Good) Desserts from the Heart of Amish Country

If you're yearning for a taste of the simple life, you've certainly come to the right place! We've compiled dozens of the best dessert recipes from *Wanda E. Brunstetter's Amish Friends Cookbook*s into one delightful edition. Recipes for homemade cakes, candies, cookies, ice cream, pies, puddings, and cobblers will transport your taste buds to the slow lane, where you'll savor authentic Amish cookery. . .and find your heart inspired by the simple life of the Plain People.

Cakes

And they gave him a piece of a cake of figs, and two clusters of raisins:
and when he had eaten, his spirit came again to him.

1 Samuel 30:12

Texas Sheet Cake

2 cups bread flour
2 cups sugar
1 cup margarine or butter, melted
3 tablespoons cocoa
1 cup water
2 eggs, beaten
½ cup sour milk
1 teaspoon baking soda
¼ teaspoon salt
1 teaspoon vanilla

FROSTING
3 tablespoons cocoa
½ cup margarine or butter, melted
6 tablespoons milk
1 teaspoon vanilla
1 pound (3½ cups) powdered sugar
1 cup nuts, chopped

Preheat oven to 350°. In large bowl, combine flour and sugar. In saucepan, mix melted margarine and cocoa; add water. Bring to a boil. Pour over flour and sugar mixture. Add eggs, milk, soda, salt, and vanilla. Mix well. Pour into greased 10x15-inch pan. Bake 25 minutes or until done. Cool. To make frosting, stir cocoa into melted margarine. Add milk and vanilla. Pour over powdered sugar and mix well. Frost cake and sprinkle with nuts.

Mrs. Leander Miller
Cashton, Wisconsin

Honey Bun Cake

1 yellow cake mix
4 eggs
⅔ cup oil
½ cup sour cream
1 cup packed brown sugar
2 teaspoons cinnamon

GLAZE
1½ cups powdered sugar
2 teaspoons vanilla
⅓ to ½ cup milk

Preheat oven to 350°. Combine cake mix, eggs, oil, and sour cream. Beat 3 minutes. Pour half of mixture into greased 9x13-inch pan. Mix brown sugar and cinnamon and sprinkle over mixture in pan. Drizzle remaining batter on top. Bake 45 to 60 minutes. Poke holes in cake with fork. Mix glaze ingredients and pour over cake while still warm.

Saloma Slabaugh
Spickard, Missouri

The best things in life are nearest: breath in your nostrils, light in your eyes, flowers at your feet, duties at your hand, the path of right just before you. Then do not grasp at the stars, but do life's plain, common work as it comes, certain that daily duties and daily bread are the sweetest things in life.
Robert Louis Stevenson

Chocolate Chip Date Nut Cake

1½ cups boiling water
1 cup finely chopped dates
1¾ teaspoons baking soda, divided
½ cup butter, softened
1½ cups sugar, divided

2 eggs
1½ cups flour
½ teaspoon salt
1 cup (6 ounces) chocolate chips
¾ cup chopped walnuts

Preheat oven to 350°. In small bowl, combine water, dates, and 1 teaspoon soda. Cool completely. In large bowl, cream butter and 1 cup sugar. Add eggs one at a time, beating well after each addition. Combine flour, salt, and remaining ¾ teaspoon soda; add to creamed mixture alternately with date mixture. Batter will be thin. Pour into greased 9x13-inch pan. Combine chocolate chips, walnuts, and remaining ½ cup sugar. Sprinkle over batter. Bake 30 to 35 minutes or until toothpick inserted in center comes out clean. Cool on wire rack.

Mrs. Joseph Zook
Rebersburg, Pennsylvania

Reduce the complexity of life by eliminating the needless wants of life, and the labors of life reduce themselves.
Edwin Way Teale

Caramel Apple Crunch Cake

1½ cups vegetable oil
3 eggs
2 cups sugar
2 teaspoons vanilla
3 cups flour
1½ teaspoons baking soda
1 teaspoon salt
1 cup chopped walnuts
1 cup coconut
3 cups chopped apples

ICING
1 stick (½ cup) butter
1 cup packed brown sugar
¼ cup milk

Preheat oven to 350°. Combine oil, eggs, sugar, and vanilla in bowl. Add flour, soda, and salt. Mix well. Stir in walnuts, coconut, and apples. Pour into greased tube pan. Bake 1½ hours. Leave cake in pan until cool; then invert onto serving plate. Combine icing ingredients in saucepan and boil 2½ minutes. Drizzle hot icing over cake.

Martha Yoder
Harrisville, Pennsylvania

Food for Thought

If you are too busy to pray, you are busier than God wants you to be.

Apple Dapple Cake

2 eggs
2 cups sugar
1 cup vegetable oil
2¾ cups flour
1 teaspoon baking soda
½ teaspoon salt
3 cups chopped apples
1 teaspoon vanilla
1 cup chopped nuts (optional)

ICING
2 tablespoons butter
1 cup packed brown sugar
¼ cup milk

Preheat oven to 350°. Combine eggs, sugar, and oil. Sift dry ingredients and add to egg mixture. Stir in apples, vanilla, and nuts (if desired). Pour into greased 9x13-inch pan and bake 30 minutes. Combine icing ingredients in saucepan and boil 2½ minutes over medium heat. Stir lightly after removing from heat. Drizzle hot icing over cake while cake is still hot.

Mrs. Jeremia Schwartz
Monroe, Indiana

Food for Thought

Many hands make work seem lighter, especially if they are proficiently skilled hands.

Maple Pudding Cake

1 cup flour
2 teaspoons baking powder
¼ teaspoon salt
½ cup sugar
½ cup milk

2 tablespoons butter or shortening, softened
1 cup chopped nuts
1 cup maple syrup
¾ cup boiling water
Whipped cream

Preheat oven to 350°. In large bowl, combine flour, baking powder, salt, and sugar. Mix in milk and butter. Stir in nuts. Spread in 2-quart baking dish. Combine maple syrup and boiling water. Pour over batter. Bake 40 to 45 minutes. Cake will rise to the top and sauce will settle to the bottom. Serve warm with whipped cream.

Susie Miller
Medford, Wisconsin

You have succeeded in life when all you really want is only what you really need.
Vernon Howard

Rhubarb Upside-Down Cake

CRUST

¼ cup butter, softened
¾ cup packed brown sugar

3 cups diced rhubarb
2 tablespoons sugar

In small bowl, combine butter and brown sugar. Spread into greased 9-inch round cake pan. Layer with rhubarb; sprinkle with sugar.

BATTER

½ cup butter, softened
1 cup sugar
2 eggs, separated
1 teaspoon vanilla
1½ cups flour

2 teaspoons baking powder
½ teaspoon salt
½ cup milk
¼ teaspoon cream of tartar

Preheat oven to 325°. Cream butter and sugar. Beat in egg yolks and vanilla. Combine flour, baking powder, and salt; add to creamed mixture alternately with milk. In small bowl, beat egg whites with cream of tartar until stiff peaks form; fold into batter. Spoon batter over rhubarb. Bake 40 to 45 minutes or until done. Serve with whipped cream.

Gwyn Auker
Elk Horn, Kentucky

Shoofly Cake

1 cup light (mild) molasses
2¼ cups boiling water
1 tablespoon baking soda

¾ cup vegetable oil
4 cups flour
1 pound light brown sugar

Preheat oven to 350°. Combine molasses, boiling water, and soda. In separate bowl, mix oil, flour, and brown sugar until mixture resembles crumbs. Reserve 1 cup crumbs for topping. Stir remaining crumbs into molasses mixture and pour into greased 9x13-inch pan. Top with reserved crumbs. Bake 40 to 45 minutes.

Marie Martin
Ephrata, Pennsylvania

Lemon Pudding Cake

8 eggs, separated
⅔ cup lemon juice
2 teaspoons lemon zest
2 tablespoons butter, melted

3 cups sugar
1 cup flour
1 teaspoon salt
3 cups milk

....

Preheat oven to 350°. Beat egg yolks, lemon juice, lemon zest, and butter. Combine sugar, flour, and salt; add to egg mixture alternately with milk. Beat egg whites until stiff and fold into batter. Pour into greased 9x13-inch pan. Set pan inside a larger pan of hot water in the oven. Bake 45 minutes.

Ellen Yoder
Scottville, Michigan

Food for Thought

Let prayer be the key to the day, and the bolt to the night.

Banana Cake

½ cup shortening
1½ cups sugar
2 eggs
1 cup mashed bananas (about 3)
1 teaspoon vanilla

2 cups flour
1 teaspoon baking soda
⅓ teaspoon salt
½ cup sour milk or buttermilk
½ cup chopped walnuts

Preheat oven to 350°. Cream shortening and sugar. Add eggs one at a time, beating well after each addition. Mix in mashed bananas and vanilla. Sift dry ingredients together and add alternately with milk. Fold in nuts. Pour into greased 9x13-inch pan and bake 45 minutes.

Mrs. Norman Miller
Clark, Missouri

Simplicity, simplicity, simplicity!
I say, let your affairs be as two or three,
and not a hundred or a thousand.
Instead of a million count half a dozen,
and keep your accounts on your thumb-nail.
HENRY DAVID THOREAU

Fudge Pudding Cake

1 cup flour
¾ cup sugar
2 tablespoons cocoa
2 teaspoons baking powder
½ teaspoon salt
½ cup milk

2 tablespoons vegetable oil
1 teaspoon vanilla
1 cup packed brown sugar
¼ cup cocoa
1¾ cups hot tap water

Preheat oven to 350°. Mix flour, sugar, cocoa, baking powder, and salt in greased 9x9-inch pan. Stir in milk, oil, and vanilla until smooth. Sprinkle with brown sugar and ¼ cup cocoa. Pour hot water over batter. Bake 40 minutes. Serve warm with vanilla ice cream, if desired.

Rachel Ann Stoltzfus
Gap, Pennsylvania

Food for Thought

When we have nothing left but God, we will find that He is enough.

Zucchini Carrot Cake

2 cups flour
2 cups sugar
2 teaspoons cinnamon
½ teaspoon salt
1 teaspoon baking powder
2 teaspoons baking soda
¾ cup vegetable oil
4 eggs
1 teaspoon vanilla
2 cups shredded zucchini
1 cup shredded carrots

CREAM CHEESE FROSTING
½ cup butter, softened
1 (8 ounce) package cream cheese, softened
3½ cups powdered sugar
1 teaspoon vanilla
1 cup chopped pecans (optional)

Preheat oven to 350°. Combine flour, sugar, cinnamon, salt, baking powder, and soda. Add oil, eggs, and vanilla; mix well. Fold in zucchini and carrots. Pour into greased 9x13-inch pan and bake 45 minutes. Cool. To make frosting, cream butter and cream cheese. Add powdered sugar and vanilla; beat until smooth. Fold in nuts, if desired.

Mrs. Levi Miller Sr.
Clark, Missouri

Coconut Blueberry Cake

2 cups flour
1 cup sugar
3 teaspoons baking powder
¼ teaspoon salt
2 eggs

1 cup milk
½ cup vegetable oil
1½ cups fresh or frozen blueberries
1 cup flaked coconut

Preheat oven to 375°. In large bowl, combine flour, sugar, baking powder, and salt. In separate bowl, beat eggs, milk, and oil; stir into dry ingredients just until moistened. Fold in blueberries. Pour into greased 9x13-inch pan. Sprinkle with coconut. Bake 22 to 24 minutes or until toothpick inserted in center comes out clean.

Regina Gingerich
LaValle, Wisconsin

*A vocabulary of truth and simplicity
will be of service throughout your life.*
Winston Churchill

Sour Cream Spice Cake

½ cup shortening
2 cups packed brown sugar
3 eggs, separated
1 cup sour cream
1¾ cups flour
2 teaspoons cinnamon
1 teaspoon cloves
1 teaspoon allspice
½ teaspoon salt
1 teaspoon vanilla

CARAMEL ICING

1 cup packed brown sugar
2 tablespoons butter
Pinch salt
3 tablespoons shortening
¼ cup milk
1½ cups powdered sugar
1 teaspoon vanilla

Preheat oven to 350°. Cream shortening and brown sugar. Add egg yolks and sour cream; mix well. Combine flour, cinnamon, cloves, allspice, and salt; add to creamed mixture and beat well. Add vanilla. Beat egg whites until stiff and fold into batter. Pour into greased 9x13-inch pan and bake 25 minutes. Cool. To make icing, combine sugar, butter, salt, and shortening in saucepan. Bring to boil; add milk. Boil 3 minutes over medium-low heat. Cool. Add powdered sugar and beat well. Stir in vanilla.

Mary Ann Yoder
Woodhull, New York

Pumpkin Sheet Cake

1 (16 ounce) can pumpkin
2 cups sugar
1 cup vegetable oil
4 eggs, lightly beaten
2 cups flour
2 teaspoons baking soda
1 teaspoon cinnamon
½ teaspoon salt

CREAM CHEESE FROSTING
5 tablespoons butter or margarine, softened
3 ounces cream cheese, softened
1 teaspoon vanilla
1¾ cups powdered sugar
3 to 4 teaspoons milk
Chopped nuts

Preheat oven to 350°. In large bowl, beat pumpkin, sugar, and oil. Add eggs and mix well. Combine flour, soda, cinnamon, and salt. Add to pumpkin mixture and mix well. Pour into greased 10x15-inch pan. Bake 25 to 30 minutes or until cake tests done. Cool. To make frosting, beat butter, cream cheese, and vanilla until smooth. Gradually add powdered sugar; mix well. Add milk until frosting reaches desired spreading consistency. Frost cake and sprinkle with nuts.

Clara Miller
Fredericktown, Ohio

Oatmeal Cake

½ cup butter
1 cup boiling water
1 cup sugar
1 cup packed brown sugar
1½ cups flour

1 cup rolled oats
1 teaspoon baking soda
Pinch salt
2 eggs
1 teaspoon vanilla

Preheat oven to 350°. Combine butter, boiling water, and sugars; let sit until butter melts. Combine flour, oats, soda, and salt; add to sugar mixture. Add eggs and vanilla; mix well. Pour into greased 8x12-inch pan and bake 30 to 35 minutes.

Mrs. Dan Swartzentruber
Newcomerstown, Ohio

Food for Thought

God does not shield us from life's storms; He shelters us in life's storms.

Candy

O taste and see that the LORD is good.

PSALM 34:8

Caramels

2 cups sugar
1¾ cups molasses
2 cups cream, divided

1 cup butter
1 teaspoon vanilla

....

Mix sugar, molasses, 1 cup cream, butter, and vanilla. Bring to a boil over low heat, stirring constantly. Add remaining 1 cup cream. Don't allow mixture to stop boiling. Boil until piece of mixture forms firm ball in cold water (250°). Pour into buttered 9x9-inch pan. When cool, cut into squares and wrap in waxed paper.

Naomi Smoker
Myerstown, Pennsylvania

*In character, in manner, in style, in all things,
the supreme excellence is simplicity.*
Henry Wadsworth Longfellow

Strawberry Divinity

3 cups sugar
¾ cup light corn syrup
¾ cup water

2 egg whites
1 (3 ounce) package strawberry gelatin
1 cup chopped nuts

Combine sugar, corn syrup, and water in heavy 3-quart saucepan. Cook over medium heat, stirring constantly, until sugar is dissolved. If sugar crystals form on sides of pan, wipe them off. Continue cooking until mixture reaches hard ball stage (252°). Meanwhile, beat egg whites until stiff but not dry. Blend gelatin into egg whites. When syrup reaches 252°, pour slowly over egg-white mixture, beating constantly on medium speed. Beat as long as possible, using wooden spoon if mixture becomes too stiff for mixer. Add nuts and spread into lightly buttered 9x9-inch pan. When cool and firm, cut into 36 pieces. Yields about 2 pounds.

Cora Hershberger
Burton, Ohio

No-Cook Fudge

2 cups powdered sugar, sifted
1 (8 ounce) package cream cheese, softened
4 ounces unsweetened chocolate, melted

½ cup chopped walnuts or pecans
1 teaspoon vanilla
Pinch salt

Gradually add powdered sugar to softened cream cheese and mix well. Thoroughly mix in warm chocolate. Stir in nuts. Add vanilla and salt. Spread in greased 8x8-inch pan. Cut and serve.

Mrs. Levi Stutzman
West Salem, Ohio

Buckeyes

2 cups (12 ounces) chocolate chips
⅓ stick paraffin
1 pound powdered sugar

1 stick (½ cup) margarine, softened
2 cups peanut butter
3 cups crisp rice cereal

. . . .

In saucepan, melt chocolate chips and paraffin over low heat. Set aside. Combine powdered sugar, margarine, peanut butter, and crisp rice cereal. Form into small balls and dip in melted chocolate mixture.

Barbara L. Weaver
Osseo, Michigan

White Chocolate Candy

1 pound white chocolate   1 cup chopped pecans or walnuts
1 cup peanut butter

In double boiler, heat chocolate until melted. Stir in peanut butter and nuts. Pour into 8x8-inch pan lined with waxed paper. When cool, remove from pan. Remove paper and cut into squares.

Rebecca Troyer
Berne, Indiana

"Think simple" as my old master used to say—
meaning reduce the whole of its parts into the simplest terms,
getting back to first principles.
Frank Lloyd Wright

Cherries 'n' Chocolate Fudge

1 (14 ounce) can sweetened condensed milk
2 cups (12 ounces) semisweet chocolate chips

½ cup coarsely chopped almonds
½ cup chopped candied cherries
1 teaspoon almond extract

Line 8x8-inch pan with foil. In medium saucepan, combine condensed milk and chocolate chips. Heat until chocolate chips are melted. Stir in almonds, cherries, and almond extract. Spread evenly in pan. Cover and chill until firm. Cut into 1-inch squares. Store covered in refrigerator.

Janine Merdian
Lacon, Illinois

Simplicity, clarity, singleness:
These are the attributes that give our lives power and vividness and joy
as they are also the marks of great art.
They seem to be the purpose of God for His whole creation.
Richard Holloway

Mints

1 (8 ounce) package cream cheese
2 pounds powdered sugar
Color paste (amount according to desired
   color)

Mint flavoring (according to taste)
1 cup sugar

....

Divide cream cheese into two equal parts and bring to room temperature. To each 4-ounce portion of cream cheese, add 1 pound of powdered sugar and knead. Add color paste with toothpick and a few drops of flavoring. Work into dough and taste for correct amount of flavor. Shape into balls; then roll in sugar and press into molds. Yields 180 mints. (Note: A food processor can be used to make this dough.)

Rosanna Zimmerman
New Holland, Pennsylvania

Food for Thought

If you can't have the best of everything, make the best of every thing you have.

Peanut Brittle

½ cup butter
1 cup light corn syrup
1 cup sugar

3 cups peanuts
2 teaspoons baking soda

....

In saucepan, combine butter, corn syrup, and sugar and cook to soft ball stage (240°). Stir in peanuts. Cook until candy thermometer reaches hard crack stage (300°). Remove from heat and quickly stir in soda; mixture will foam. Pour over foil and let cool before breaking up.

Saloma Slabaugh
Spickard, Missouri

Food for Thought

Faith is not belief without proof but trust without reservation.

Mocha Truffles

4 cups (24 ounces) semisweet chocolate
   chips
1 (8 ounce) package cream cheese
3 tablespoons instant coffee granules

2 teaspoons water
Additional semisweet chocolate chips,
   melted

In saucepan, melt chocolate chips. Add cream cheese, coffee granules, and water; mix well. Chill until firm enough to shape. Shape into 1-inch balls and place on baking sheet lined with waxed paper. Chill 1 to 2 hours or until firm. Dip in additional melted chocolate. Yields about 5½ dozen truffles.

Sarah Troyer
Mercer, Pennsylvania

Rocky Road Candy

½ cup butter or margarine
½ cup powdered sugar
1 egg, beaten

1 cup chocolate or butterscotch chips
3 or 4 cups miniature marshmallows
10 graham cracker squares

In double boiler, combine butter, powdered sugar, egg, and chocolate chips. Heat and stir until melted. Cool slightly. Add marshmallows. Line bottom of ungreased 8x8-inch pan with graham crackers. Pour melted mixture on top. Cool. Cut into squares.

Barbara Miller
Port Washington, Ohio

Date Balls

1 egg, beaten
1 cup sugar
1 stick (½ cup) butter or margarine
1 cup cut-up dates

3 cups crisp rice cereal
1 to 2 cups flaked coconut

Combine egg, sugar, butter, and dates in saucepan. Cook 6 minutes over low heat. Pour over crisp rice cereal and stir. Shape into balls; then roll in coconut.

Mrs. Eli Miller
Chili, Wisconsin

Food for Thought
When I come to the end of my rope, God is there to take over.

Marbled Orange Fudge

¾ cup butter (no substitutes)
3 cups sugar
¾ cup whipping cream
1 package vanilla or white chocolate chips

1 (7 ounce) jar marshmallow crème
3 teaspoons orange extract
12 drops yellow food coloring
5 drops red food coloring

In heavy saucepan, combine butter, sugar, and whipping cream. Cook and stir over low heat until sugar is dissolved. Bring to a boil; cook and stir 4 minutes. Remove from heat; stir in chips and marshmallow crème. Remove 1 cup and set aside. Add orange extract and colorings to remaining mixture. Stir until blended. Pour into greased 9x13-inch pan. Drop reserved mixture by tablespoons on top and cut through with a knife to swirl.

Linda Peachey
Beaver, Ohio

From the simple seeds of childlike faith,
we reap the lovely harvest of God's reassuring presence in our lives.
Unknown

Goat's Milk Fudge

3 cups sugar
1 cup goat's milk
¼ cup light corn syrup
1 tablespoon butter

1 pound chocolate or white almond bark
   coating
1 teaspoon vanilla or maple flavoring
Chopped nuts (optional)

In saucepan, combine sugar, milk, and corn syrup; bring to a boil. Cook until almost to soft ball stage (240°). Remove pan from heat and set in bowl of cold water until mixture becomes thick around the edges. Add butter and almond bark coating; stir until glossy. Add vanilla or maple flavoring. Stir in nuts, if desired.

Mrs. David Sommers
La Plata, Missouri

Food for Thought
If we let God guide, He will provide.

Peanut Butter Fudge

1 cup margarine

1 cup crunchy peanut butter

4 cups powdered sugar

1 teaspoon vanilla

In saucepan, melt margarine and add peanut butter, powdered sugar, and vanilla. Beat well until smooth. Pour into greased 8x8-inch pan. Refrigerate 3 hours.

Marie Troyer
Mercer, Pennsylvania

Peppermint Patties

½ cup warm mashed potatoes (mashed
   with milk only)
1 tablespoon shortening

3½ cups powdered sugar
7 drops peppermint extract
Dark sweet chocolate, melted

....

Beat all ingredients except chocolate until smooth. Add additional powdered sugar if needed to reach desired consistency. Shape into patties and freeze. Coat patties with melted chocolate while frozen.

This recipe won a first-place ribbon at the Malheur County Fair in Ontario, Oregon. It also won the grand prize in the candy division.

Bertha Stauffer
Mechanicsville, Missouri

Contentment is. . .the realization of how much you already have.
Unknown

Coconut Bonbons

2 cups sugar
2 cups light corn syrup
¼ cup butter or margarine

2 cups flaked coconut
Semisweet chocolate chips, melted

Combine sugar, corn syrup, and butter in saucepan; bring to a boil. Cook until mixture reaches hard ball stage (252°). Remove from heat and stir in coconut. Cool and shape into balls. Dip in melted chocolate.

Barbara Miller
Port Washington, Ohio

Food for Thought
Every child of God has a special place in His plan.

Cookies & Bars

How sweet are thy words unto my taste!
yea, sweeter than honey to my mouth!

Psalm 119:103

Peanut Butter Fingers

½ cup butter or margarine
½ cup sugar
½ cup packed brown sugar
1 egg
⅓ cup peanut butter
½ teaspoon baking soda
¼ teaspoon salt
½ teaspoon vanilla
1 cup rolled oats
1 cup flour
1 cup (6 ounces) chocolate chips

PEANUT BUTTER FROSTING
½ cup powdered sugar
¼ cup peanut butter
2 to 4 tablespoons milk

Preheat oven to 350°. Cream butter and sugars. Blend in egg and peanut butter. Add soda, salt, vanilla, oats, and flour. Mix well. Spread in greased 9x13-inch pan and bake 20 to 25 minutes. Sprinkle chocolate chips over crust while still hot. Cool. To make frosting, combine powdered sugar and peanut butter and stir in enough milk to reach desired spreading consistency. Frost and cut into bars for serving.

Amanda Stutzman
Apple Creek, Ohio

Maple Chocolate Walnut Bars

CRUST
1½ cups flour
⅔ cup sugar
¾ cup cold butter or margarine
½ teaspoon salt
1 egg, beaten

FILLING
1 cup chocolate chips
1 (14 ounce) can sweetened condensed milk
1½ teaspoons maple flavoring
1 egg, beaten
2 cups chopped walnuts

Preheat oven to 350°. In large bowl, mix flour, sugar, butter, and salt until crumbly. Stir in egg. Press evenly into greased 9x13-inch pan. Bake 25 minutes. Sprinkle chocolate chips over baked crust. Combine condensed milk, maple flavoring, and egg; stir in walnuts. Pour over baked crust and bake 20 minutes longer or until golden brown. Cool. Cut into bars.

Alice Beechy
Pittsford, Michigan

Our life is frittered away by detail. . . . Simplify, simplify, simplify!
Henry David Thoreau

Pecan Squares

CRUST
3 cups flour
½ cup sugar
1 cup butter or margarine, softened
½ teaspoon salt

FILLING
4 eggs
1½ cups light or dark corn syrup
1½ cups sugar
3 tablespoons butter or margarine, melted
1½ teaspoons vanilla
2½ cups chopped pecans

Preheat oven to 350°. Blend flour, sugar, butter, and salt until mixture forms coarse crumbs. Press into greased 9x13-inch pan. Bake 20 minutes. Meanwhile, combine eggs, corn syrup, sugar, butter, and vanilla. Stir in pecans. Spread filling evenly over hot crust and bake 25 minutes longer or until set. Cool and cut into squares. Store in airtight container. Yields 2 dozen squares.

Mary Schwartz
Monroe, Indiana

Boyfriend Cookies

1 cup butter, softened
¾ cup sugar
¾ cup packed brown sugar
3 eggs
1 teaspoon vanilla

¼ cup whole-wheat flour
¼ cup soy flour
3½ cups quick oats
1½ cups salted peanuts, coarsely chopped
1 cup carob chips

Preheat oven to 350°. Cream butter and sugars. Add eggs and vanilla, beating until fluffy. Sift flours and add to creamed mixture. Fold in oats, peanuts, and carob chips. Drop by teaspoons onto greased baking sheet and bake 8 to 10 minutes. Yields 7 to 8 dozen cookies.

Emma A. Troyer
New Wilmington, Pennsylvania

Act with God in the greatest simplicity.
Speak to Him frankly and plainly.
Brother Lawrence

Date Pinwheel Cookies

FILLING
2 pounds chopped dates
1 cup sugar
1 cup water

DOUGH
1⅓ cups packed brown sugar
⅔ cup shortening
2 eggs, beaten
2½ cups flour
¾ teaspoon baking soda
½ teaspoon salt
½ teaspoon cinnamon

Preheat oven to 400°. To make filling, combine dates, sugar, and water in saucepan. Cook over medium-low heat, stirring constantly, until mixture forms a smooth paste. Cool. In large bowl, cream brown sugar and shortening. Add eggs and beat until mixture is light and fluffy. Combine flour, soda, salt, and cinnamon. Gradually add to creamed mixture and stir until soft dough forms. Divide dough into 4 parts. Cover with waxed paper and chill thoroughly. Working with one portion of dough at a time and keeping remaining dough cool, roll out in rectangle ⅛ inch thick. Spread date filling to within ¼ inch of edges; roll up jelly roll style, starting with long side. Pinch edge to seal. Wrap each roll and refrigerate overnight. Remove from refrigerator as needed. With sharp knife, cut in ¼-inch slices and bake on lightly greased baking sheet 8 to 10 minutes or until light golden brown.

Susan Weaver
Osseo, Michigan

Swedish Butter Cookies

1 cup butter, softened (no substitutes)
1 cup sugar
2 teaspoons maple syrup

2 cups flour
1 teaspoon baking soda

Preheat oven to 300°. Cream butter and sugar. Add maple syrup and stir well. Combine flour and soda and add to creamed mixture. Shape into balls and place on ungreased baking sheet. Bake 25 minutes or until lightly browned.

Linda E. Peachey
Beaver, Ohio

Maple Nut Cookies

2 cups packed brown sugar
1 cup butter
3 eggs
1¼ tablespoons maple flavoring
¾ cup milk
4 cups flour
2 teaspoons baking soda
¼ teaspoon salt
¾ cup chopped nuts

FROSTING
¼ cup butter
1 egg, beaten
1 teaspoon maple flavoring
2¼ cups powdered sugar
2 teaspoons water

Preheat oven to 350°. Cream brown sugar and butter. Add eggs, maple flavoring, and milk; beat well. Combine flour, soda, and salt; add to creamed mixture. Fold in nuts. Drop by heaping teaspoons onto greased baking sheet and bake 8 to 10 minutes. Blend frosting ingredients until smooth. Frost cookies when cool.

Lizzie Yoder
Fredericksburg, Ohio

Food for Thought

No person can do everything, but each one can do something.

Old-Fashioned Ginger Cookies

2 cups molasses
1 cup sugar
2 cups shortening
10 cups flour (half pastry and half bread flour)
1 teaspoon salt

2 tablespoons baking soda
1 teaspoon ginger
1 teaspoon cinnamon
2 cups sour milk or buttermilk
1 egg, beaten

Preheat oven to 350°. In saucepan, heat molasses and sugar. Add shortening and stir until smooth. Remove from heat. Sift together flour, salt, soda, ginger, and cinnamon. Add to molasses mixture alternately with milk. Stir until smooth dough forms. Work with hands 5 minutes. Chill. Roll out to ½ inch thick and cut into shapes. Glaze cookies with beaten egg. Bake on greased baking sheet 20 to 25 minutes. Yields 8 dozen cookies.

Ruth S. Martin
Selins Grove, Pennsylvania

Enjoy the little things, for one day you may look back and realize they were the big things.
Robert Brault

Coconut Oatmeal Cookies

2 cups flour
1½ cups sugar, divided
1 teaspoon baking powder
1 teaspoon baking soda
½ teaspoon salt
1 cup packed brown sugar

1 cup shortening
2 eggs
½ teaspoon vanilla
1½ cups quick oats
1 cup flaked coconut
1 cup chopped walnuts

Preheat oven to 375°. Sift together flour, 1 cup sugar, baking powder, soda, and salt. Add brown sugar, shortening, eggs, and vanilla. Beat well. Stir in oats, coconut, and walnuts. Shape into small balls and dip tops in ½ cup sugar. Place on ungreased baking sheet and bake 12 to 14 minutes. Yields about 5½ dozen cookies.

Mary Alice Kulp
Narvon, Pennsylvania

Buttermilk Cookies

2 cups butter or margarine
3 cups packed brown sugar
1 cup sugar
3 eggs
4 teaspoons baking powder

4 teaspoons baking soda
4 teaspoons vanilla
1½ cups buttermilk or sour milk
8 cups flour

Preheat oven to 350°. Cream butter and sugars. Add eggs, baking powder, soda, and vanilla; mix well. Add milk alternately with flour until well blended. Drop by teaspoons onto well-greased baking sheet and bake 11 to 13 minutes. Let set for 5 minutes before removing from baking sheet. (Note: To sour milk, add 1 teaspoon vinegar to each cup of milk.)

This recipe won a first-place ribbon at the Malheur County Fair in Ontario, Oregon.

Emma Raber
Holmesville, Ohio

Food for Thought
You can't speak a kind word too soon.

Maple Syrup Cookies

1 teaspoon baking soda
1 tablespoon milk
1 egg
½ cup plus 2 tablespoons shortening
1 cup maple syrup
3 cups flour

3 teaspoons baking powder
½ teaspoon salt
1 teaspoon vanilla
1⅓ cups (8 ounces) semisweet chocolate
  chips

Preheat oven to 350°. In small cup, dissolve soda in milk and set aside. Cream egg, shortening, and maple syrup. Add flour, baking powder, salt, vanilla, and soda mixture; blend well. Stir in chocolate chips. Drop by teaspoons onto greased baking sheet and bake 12 to 15 minutes.

Mattie Ann Miller
Medford, Wisconsin

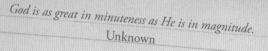

God is as great in minuteness as He is in magnitude.
Unknown

Frosted Rhubarb Cookies

1 cup shortening
1½ cups packed brown sugar
2 eggs
3 cups flour
1 teaspoon baking soda
½ teaspoon salt
1½ cups diced rhubarb
¾ cup flaked coconut

CREAM CHEESE FROSTING
3 ounces cream cheese
1 tablespoon butter, softened
1½ cups powdered sugar
3 teaspoons vanilla

Preheat oven to 350°. In large bowl, cream shortening and brown sugar. Beat in eggs. Combine flour, soda, and salt; add to creamed mixture. Fold in rhubarb and coconut. Drop by rounded tablespoons 2 inches apart onto greased baking sheet. Bake 10 to 14 minutes or until golden brown. Blend frosting ingredients until smooth. Frost cookies when cool.

Gwyn Auker
Elk Horn, Kentucky

Lemon Bars

CRUST
1 cup butter or margarine
2 cups flour
½ cup powdered sugar
Pinch salt

FILLING
4 eggs, beaten
2 cups sugar
6 tablespoons lemon juice
4 tablespoons flour

TOPPING
¼ to ½ cup powdered sugar

Preheat oven to 350°. Mix crust ingredients and press into 9x13-inch pan. Bake 15 to 20 minutes. Meanwhile, beat eggs, sugar, lemon juice, and flour. Pour over baked crust and bake 20 to 30 minutes longer. Cool slightly and sift powdered sugar over bars.

Emma E. Raber
Holmesville, Ohio

Food for Thought
Don't overlook life's small joys while searching for the big ones.

Apple Butter Bars

1½ cups flour
1 teaspoon baking soda
1 teaspoon salt
2½ cups quick oats

1½ cups sugar
1 cup margarine, softened
1½ cups apple butter

Preheat oven to 350°. Sift flour, soda, and salt in large bowl. Add oats and sugar. Stir in margarine and mix well. Press half of mixture into greased 9x13-inch pan. Top with apple butter. Sprinkle with remaining crumbs; press gently with spoon. Bake 55 minutes or until lightly browned.

Nelson and Miriam Hershberger
Calhoun, Illinois

Food for Thought

Happy hearts make happy homes.

Grassroot Dream Cookies

½ cup margarine
½ cup sugar
½ cup packed brown sugar
1 egg
¾ teaspoon vanilla
1 cup flour

1 teaspoon baking powder
¼ teaspoon baking soda
¼ teaspoon salt
½ cup rolled oats
1 cup cornflakes
½ cup flaked coconut

Preheat oven to 325°. Cream margarine and sugars. Add egg and vanilla; blend until smooth. Sift flour, baking powder, soda, and salt; add to creamed mixture. Stir in oats, cornflakes, and coconut. Drop by teaspoons onto lightly greased baking sheet. Bake 12 to 15 minutes. Yields 5 dozen crisp 2-inch cookies.

Susanna Schrock
Wheatland, Missouri

Food for Thought

Find contentment in enjoying the present season instead of dreaming about the next.

Raisin Molasses Cookies

2 cups raisins
1 cup shortening
½ cup sugar
2 eggs
1½ cups molasses
4 cups flour

3 teaspoons baking powder
½ teaspoon baking soda
1 teaspoon salt
2 teaspoons cinnamon
2 teaspoons ginger

Rinse and drain raisins. Cream shortening and sugar. Add eggs and beat well. Blend in molasses. Sift flour, baking powder, soda, salt, cinnamon, and ginger. Blend into creamed mixture. Stir in raisins. Drop by teaspoons onto greased baking sheet and bake 15 to 18 minutes. Yields about 6 dozen cookies.

Martha Byler
Spartansburg, Pennsylvania

God, of Your goodness, give me Yourself,
for You are enough for me.
And only in You do I have everything.
Julian of Norwich

Ice Cream, Toppings & Frozen Desserts

*If the L*ORD *delight in us, then he will bring us into this land. . .*
a land which floweth with milk and honey.

NUMBERS 14:8

Frozen Strawberry Pudding

1 (8 ounce) package cream cheese, softened
¾ cup sugar
1 quart strawberries, sliced

1 (8 ounce) carton frozen whipped
   topping, thawed
3 cups miniature marshmallows

Blend cream cheese and sugar until smooth. Add strawberries and whipped topping. Stir in marshmallows and freeze.

Dianna Yoder
Goshen, Indiana

To be refreshed by a morning walk or an evening saunter. . . to be thrilled by the stars at night; to be elated over a bird's nest or a wildflower in spring— these are some of the rewards of the simple life.
John Burroughs

Homemade Popsicles

2 (6 ounce) packages gelatin (any flavor)   4 cups boiling water
2 cups sugar   4 cups cold water
2 packages Kool-Aid (any flavor)

Combine all ingredients except cold water and mix well. Add cold water. Pour into molds and freeze.

Mary Ann Yoder
Woodhull, New York

Butter Pecan Ice Cream

1 tablespoon margarine, melted
⅔ cup packed brown sugar
½ cup chopped pecans
½ teaspoon maple flavoring
1 (4 serving) package vanilla instant
   pudding

1 (4 serving) package butterscotch instant
   pudding
1 pint cream
Milk

Mix all ingredients except milk and put into 1-gallon ice-cream freezer. Add enough milk to fill freezer. Process until frozen.

Jacob Schwartz
Portland, Indiana

Ice Cream Jell-O

1 (3 ounce) package gelatin (any flavor)   Vanilla ice cream, softened

....

Prepare your favorite flavored gelatin as directed, but instead of stirring in the amount of cold water called for in package directions, stir in that amount of vanilla ice cream. Let set.

Sarah B. Eicher
Geneva, Indiana

Food for Thought

There is no scale or chart on earth to measure what a true friend is worth.

Homemade Fudgesicles

2 cups milk
1 (4 serving) package chocolate instant
  pudding

¼ cup sugar
1 cup evaporated milk or ¼ cup cream

....

Stir milk into pudding mix. Add sugar and evaporated milk or cream. Pour into molds and freeze.

Martha Yoder
Harrisville, Pennsylvania

Eliminate physical clutter.
More importantly, eliminate spiritual clutter.
D. H. Mondfleur

Ice Cream Pudding

1 gallon vanilla ice cream
2 packages chocolate sandwich cookies

1 (16 ounce) carton frozen whipped
  topping, thawed

....

Melt ice cream so you can stir it well. Grind cookies and add to ice cream. Mix in whipped topping. Pour into 11x15-inch pan. Freeze.

Leah Schwartz
Portland, Indiana

Food for Thought
Have your harvest tools ready, and God will find work for you.

Frozen Mocha Marble Loaf

4 cups finely crushed chocolate sandwich
    cookies (about 44 cookies)
6 tablespoons butter or margarine, melted
2 (8 ounce) packages cream cheese,
    softened
2 (14 ounce) cans sweetened condensed
    milk

2 teaspoons vanilla
1 (16 ounce) container frozen whipped
    topping, thawed
4 tablespoons instant coffee granules
2 tablespoons hot water
1 cup chocolate syrup

Combine cookie crumbs and butter. Press into lightly greased 9x13-inch pan. Beat cream cheese until light. Add condensed milk and vanilla; mix well. Fold in whipped topping. Set aside half of mixture. Dissolve coffee granules in hot water and fold into remaining cream cheese mixture. Fold in chocolate syrup. Spoon half of chocolate mixture over crust and top with half of cream cheese mixture. Repeat layers. Cover and freeze 6 hours or overnight.

Elizabeth Shrock
Jamestown, Pennsylvania

Vanilla Ice Cream

1 quart cream
8 eggs
2 (3 ounce) packages vanilla instant
    pudding mix

2 cans evaporated milk
½ cup packed brown sugar
1½ cups sugar
Milk

....

Whip cream. In separate bowl, beat eggs well; add to whipped cream. Prepare pudding according to package directions and add to whipped cream and eggs. Add evaporated milk and pour into 2-gallon ice-cream freezer. Add enough milk to fill freezer. Process until frozen.

Sarah Miller
Dundee, Ohio

Sherbet

2 (6 ounce) packages gelatin (any flavor)   ½ cup sugar
2 cups hot water   2 quarts milk

....

Dissolve gelatin in water and chill until partially set. Add sugar and milk; beat well. Pour into ice-cream freezer and process until frozen.

Lovina Hershberger
Dalton, Ohio

When we stop the mad rush, when we say no to some of our many responsibilities and take the time to come quietly into God's presence, then, in that simple, quiet moment, He will breathe His peace into our hearts.
Ellyn Sanna

Hand-Cranked French Strawberry Ice Cream

6 egg yolks
2 cups milk
1 cup sugar
Pinch salt

4 cups heavy cream
2 cups crushed strawberries
1 tablespoon lemon juice

Combine egg yolks, milk, sugar, and salt in double boiler and heat until mixture forms thick custard. Cook until mixture coats the back of a wooden spoon evenly. Allow to cool. Add heavy cream. Pour into ice-cream freezer and crank until half frozen. Add crushed strawberries and lemon juice and continue to crank until frozen. Allow to stand a few hours before serving. Yields 2½ quarts.

Mollie Stoltzfus
Charlotte Hall, Maryland

The key to happiness belongs to everyone on earth who recognizes simple things as treasures of great worth.
Unknown

School Ice Cream

9 eggs
3 tablespoons unflavored gelatin
3¾ cups milk, divided
2 (3 ounce) packages instant pudding
  (any flavor)

2 quarts cream or milk
2½ cups sugar
½ cup packed brown sugar
2 tablespoons vanilla

In large bowl, beat eggs well. Soak gelatin in ¾ cup cold milk. Heat remaining 3 cups milk; add gelatin mixture and stir until dissolved. Add pudding mix, cream, sugars, and vanilla to beaten eggs; beat well. Pour into ice-cream freezer and process until frozen.

Lena Byler
Atlantic, Pennsylvania

Food for Thought
Trust God to move your mountains, but keep on digging.

Chocolate Sauce

1 cup sugar
2 tablespoons butter or margarine
¼ cup cream or milk

4 tablespoons light corn syrup or maple
  syrup
2 scant tablespoons cocoa

....

Combine all ingredients in saucepan and bring to a boil. Cook 3 minutes and serve over ice cream.

Mattie Ann Miller
Medford, Wisconsin

Food for Thought

It's impossible to drive in the wrong direction and arrive at the right destination.

Butterscotch Topping

3 teaspoons butter
1 cup sugar
1 cup packed brown sugar

½ teaspoon salt
½ cup milk
1 teaspoon vanilla

Melt butter in saucepan and add sugars, salt, and milk. Cook 2 minutes. Add vanilla.

Lydia Troyer
Mercer, Pennsylvania

Frozen Fudge

1½ cups milk
½ cup cream
½ cup sugar

3 tablespoons cocoa
½ teaspoon vanilla
Pinch salt

....

Combine all ingredients and blend until smooth. Pour into ice-cube tray and freeze overnight or until hard. Thaw 5 to 10 minutes before serving.

Clara Yoder
Windsor, Missouri

Pies

Whether therefore ye eat, or drink,
or whatsoever ye do, do all to the glory of God.

1 Corinthians 10:31

Country Fair Pie

½ cup butter or margarine, melted
1 cup sugar
½ cup flour
2 eggs
1 teaspoon vanilla

1 cup (6 ounces) semisweet chocolate chips
½ cup butterscotch chips
1 cup chopped nuts
1 (9 inch) unbaked pastry shell

Preheat oven to 325°. Beat butter, sugar, flour, eggs, and vanilla until well blended. Stir in chips and nuts. Pour into unbaked pastry shell. Bake 1 hour or until golden brown. Cool on wire rack.

Susan Schwartz
Berne, Indiana

Apple Cream Pie

3 cups apples, finely chopped
1 cup packed brown sugar
¼ teaspoon salt

1 rounded tablespoon flour
1 cup cream
1 (9 inch) unbaked pastry shell

Preheat oven to 450°. Mix apples, brown sugar, salt, flour, and cream. Spread in unbaked pastry shell. Bake 15 minutes. Reduce heat to 325° and bake 30 to 40 minutes longer. When pie is about half done, push top apples down to soften.

Mandy R. Schwartz
Portland, Indiana

Food for Thought

Keep looking up, for God is looking down.

Angel Cream Pie

1 cup half-and-half
1 cup heavy whipping cream
½ cup sugar
⅛ teaspoon salt

2 rounded tablespoons flour
1 teaspoon vanilla
2 egg whites, stiffly beaten
1 (9 inch) unbaked pastry shell

Preheat oven to 350°. In saucepan, combine half-and-half and whipping cream. Warm slightly. Turn off heat and add sugar, salt, and flour; beat with whisk. Add vanilla and fold in stiffly beaten egg whites. Pour into unbaked pastry shell. Bake 45 minutes or until just a little shaky.

Betty Miller
Goshen, Indiana

Seeing our Father in everything makes life one long thanksgiving and gives a rest of heart.
Hannah Whitall Smith

Sour Cream Peach Pie

1 egg, beaten
½ teaspoon salt
½ teaspoon vanilla
1 cup sour cream
¾ cup sugar
2 tablespoons flour
2½ cups sliced fresh peaches
1 (9 inch) unbaked pastry shell

TOPPING
½ cup butter
⅓ cup sugar
⅓ cup flour
1 teaspoon cinnamon

Preheat oven to 375°. Combine egg, salt, vanilla, sour cream, sugar, and flour. Stir in peaches. Pour into unbaked pastry shell and bake 30 minutes or until pie is slightly brown. Remove from oven. Combine topping ingredients, spread on top of pie, and bake 15 minutes longer.

Sylvia Miller
Rossiter, Pennsylvania

God loves and cares for us, even to the least event and smallest need of life.
Henry Edward Manning

Funny Cake Pie

CAKE BATTER
1¼ cups flour
¾ cup sugar
2 teaspoons baking powder
¼ cup shortening
1 egg
½ cup milk
½ teaspoon vanilla

BASE
1 cup sugar
¼ cup cocoa
¾ cup hot water
1 teaspoon vanilla
1 (9 inch) unbaked pastry shell

Preheat oven to 350°. Combine cake batter ingredients and set aside. Mix sugar, cocoa, water, and vanilla and pour into unbaked pastry shell. Carefully pour cake batter on top. Bake 45 minutes.

Miriam Brunstetter
Easton, Pennsylvania

Food for Thought
Life without Christ is a hopeless end. With Christ, it's an endless hope.

Coconut Oatmeal Pie

1 cup light corn syrup
½ cup packed brown sugar
⅓ cup butter, melted
1 teaspoon vanilla
⅓ teaspoon salt

3 eggs, beaten
½ cup flaked coconut
½ cup quick oats
1 (9 inch) unbaked pastry shell

Preheat oven to 350°. Combine all ingredients in order given and mix well. Pour into unbaked pastry shell and bake 30 to 35 minutes or until pie tests done.

Mrs. John Miller
Navarre, Ohio

Shoofly Pie

CRUMB MIXTURE

4 cups flour

2 cups sugar

3 tablespoons butter

3 tablespoons lard or shortening

1 teaspoon cinnamon

¾ teaspoon nutmeg

¾ teaspoon ginger

Pinch salt

Blend all ingredients until mixture forms crumbs. (Note: Butter and lard [or shortening] tablespoon measurements should be level. Crumbs will be dry.)

FILLING

2 cups cane molasses

2 cups warm water

1 tablespoon baking soda

4 (9 inch) unbaked pastry shells

Preheat oven to 350°. Combine molasses, water, and baking soda. Divide mixture equally into unbaked pastry shells. Divide crumbs and sprinkle evenly on top of filling in pastry shells; let stand for 10 minutes. Bake 30 to 40 minutes or until done.

Mattie Hershberger
Heuvelton, New York

Food for Thought

Remedy for discouragement: Reach up as far as you can, and God will reach down the rest of the way.

Lemon Shoofly Pie

CRUMB MIXTURE
1½ cups flour

½ cup sugar

½ cup shortening or butter, softened

½ teaspoon baking soda

Blend all ingredients until mixture forms crumbs.

FILLING
1 egg

Zest and juice of 2 lemons

2 tablespoons flour

½ cup sugar

½ cup molasses

¾ cup boiling water

1 (9 inch) unbaked pastry shell

Preheat oven to 350°. Combine filling ingredients and pour into unbaked pastry shell. Sprinkle crumbs evenly on top of filling. Bake 45 to 60 minutes.

This recipe won a first-place ribbon at the Malheur County Fair in Ontario, Oregon.

Mrs. Henry Leid
Elkton, Kentucky

Vanilla Crumb Pie

CRUMB MIXTURE

2 cups flour
1 cup packed brown sugar
½ cup lard

1 teaspoon cream of tartar
½ teaspoon baking powder

Blend all ingredients until mixture forms crumbs.

FILLING

1 cup packed brown sugar
1 cup light corn syrup
2 cups water
2 tablespoons flour
1 egg

½ teaspoon cream of tartar
1 teaspoon vanilla
1 teaspoon baking soda
3 (9 inch) unbaked pastry shells

Preheat oven to 375°. In saucepan, combine brown sugar, corn syrup, water, and flour. Heat to boiling and boil 1 minute; set aside. In large bowl, beat egg, cream of tartar, vanilla, and baking soda; add to cooked mixture. Divide mixture equally into unbaked pastry shells. Divide crumbs and sprinkle evenly on top of filling in pastry shells. Bake 45 minutes.

Mahala Miller
Medford, Wisconsin

Pilgrim Pie

¼ cup margarine
1 cup sugar
2 eggs
1 cup light corn syrup
½ cup water

1 teaspoon vanilla
1 cup flaked coconut
1 cup rolled oats
½ teaspoon salt
1 (9 inch) unbaked pastry shell

Preheat oven to 450°. Cream margarine and sugar. Add remaining ingredients and mix well. Pour into unbaked pastry shell. Bake at 450° for 10 minutes; reduce heat to 350° and bake 30 minutes longer.

Mrs. Chris Beachy
McIntire, Iowa

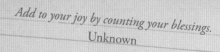

Add to your joy by counting your blessings.
Unknown

Perfect Pumpkin Pie

1 cup pumpkin or squash, cooked
1½ cups packed brown sugar
1 teaspoon salt
½ teaspoon allspice
½ teaspoon cloves
1 teaspoon cinnamon

4 tablespoons flour
4 egg yolks
4 cups milk
1 teaspoon vanilla
3 egg whites, stiffly beaten
2 (9 inch) unbaked pastry shells

Preheat oven to 375°. Combine pumpkin, brown sugar, salt, allspice, cloves, cinnamon, flour, egg yolks, milk, and vanilla until well blended. Fold in stiffly beaten egg whites. Pour into unbaked pastry shells. Bake 1 hour or until knife inserted in center comes out clean.

Mrs. Harvey R. Miller
South Dayton, New York

Rhubarb Cream Pie

2 tablespoons butter
2 cups diced rhubarb
½ cup water
1¼ cups sugar, divided
2 heaping tablespoons cornstarch
⅛ teaspoon salt
2 eggs, separated
¼ cup cream or rich milk
1 (9 inch) baked pastry shell

MERINGUE
6 tablespoons sugar
1 teaspoon lemon juice

Preheat oven to 400°. In large saucepan, melt butter; add rhubarb, water, and 1 cup sugar. Cook slowly until rhubarb is tender. In mixing bowl, combine ¼ cup sugar, cornstarch, salt, egg yolks, and cream. Add to rhubarb mixture and cook until thick. Pour into baked pastry shell. To make meringue, beat egg whites until stiff. Add 6 tablespoons sugar and 1 teaspoon lemon juice. Pile on top of pie. Bake 8 to 10 minutes or until lightly browned.

Mrs. Miller
Morley, Michigan

Food for Thought
Patience is a word that carries a lot of wait.

Raisin Cream Pie

3 cups milk
1 cup sugar
3 heaping tablespoons flour
¾ teaspoon salt
6 egg yolks
¼ cup butter or margarine

1 cup cooked raisins
3 teaspoons vanilla
2 (9 inch) baked pastry shells
1 (12 ounce) carton frozen whipped
   topping, thawed

Heat milk in saucepan. In mixing bowl, combine sugar, flour, and salt. Add egg yolks and enough milk to form a smooth paste. Add paste mixture to heated milk and stir constantly until thick. Remove from heat and add butter, cooked raisins, and vanilla. Cool. Pour into baked pastry shells. Top with whipped topping.

Anna Beechy
Topeka, Indiana

The private and personal blessings we enjoy deserve the thanksgiving of a whole life.
Jeremy Taylor

Lemon Sponge Pie

9 eggs, separated
3½ cups sugar
9 tablespoons flour
Pinch salt

Zest and juice of 3 lemons
4 tablespoons butter
6 cups milk, scalded
4 (9 inch) unbaked pastry shells

Preheat oven to 425°. Combine egg yolks, sugar, flour, and salt; mix well. Add lemon zest, lemon juice, butter, and scalded milk; mix well. Beat egg whites until stiff and fold into milk mixture. Pour into unbaked pastry shells. Bake at 425° for 15 minutes; reduce heat to 325° and bake until filling is firm.

Ida Miller
Medford, Wisconsin

*If you can eat today, enjoy the sunlight today,
mix good cheer with friends today, enjoy it and bless God for it.*
Henry Ward Beecher

Funeral Pie

1 cup raisins
2 cups hot water
1¼ cups sugar
4 tablespoons flour
1 egg, well beaten

Zest and juice of 1 lemon
¼ teaspoon salt
1 tablespoon butter
1 (8 inch) unbaked pastry shell and pastry
   strips for lattice top

Preheat oven to 450°. Wash raisins and soak in hot water for 1 hour or longer. Drain. Add remaining ingredients and mix thoroughly. Cook in double boiler until thickened. Cool. Pour into pastry shell and weave pastry strips over filling to make lattice top. Bake at 450° for 10 minutes; reduce heat to 350° and continue baking until nicely browned.

Esther Stauffer
Port Trevorton, Pennsylvania

Food for Thought

Blessed are those who give without remembering and receive without forgetting.

Key Lime Pie

CRUST

1⅓ cups graham cracker crumbs   6 tablespoons butter, melted

Preheat oven to 350°. Mix graham cracker crumbs and butter. Press onto sides and bottom of 9-inch pie pan. Bake 5 minutes. Cool completely.

FILLING

3 egg yolks   ½ cup fresh lime juice
1 (14 ounce) can sweetened condensed   1 teaspoon lime zest
  milk   1 cup heavy cream

Beat egg yolks until thick, about 4 minutes. Beat in condensed milk, lime juice, and lime zest. Pour into cooled graham cracker crust. Cover and refrigerate at least 4 hours. Before serving, beat heavy cream until stiff (do not sweeten) and spoon over pie.

Mollie Stoltzfus
Charlotte Hall, Maryland

Puddings & Cobblers

The LORD is my portion, saith my soul;
therefore will I hope in him.

LAMENTATIONS 3:24

Drumstick Pudding

CRUST
1½ cups graham cracker crumbs

¼ cup margarine, melted

¼ cup sugar

Mix graham cracker crumbs, margarine, and sugar. Press into 9x13-inch pan.

FILLING
2 (8 ounce) packages cream cheese, softened

1 (16 ounce) carton frozen whipped topping, thawed

1 cup powdered sugar

¼ cup peanut butter

1 (6 serving) package chocolate instant pudding

1 (4 serving) package vanilla instant pudding

5 cups milk

Chopped nuts (optional)

Mix cream cheese, whipped topping, powdered sugar, and peanut butter and spread over crust. Prepare pudding mixes according to package directions. Layer chocolate and vanilla on top of cream cheese mixture. Sprinkle with chopped nuts if desired. Tastes like a Drumstick ice-cream cone.

Ella Detweiler
Atlantic, Pennsylvania

Oreo Pudding

FIRST LAYER
1 (1 pound) package Oreo cookies

Crush Oreos. Reserve some crumbs for topping. Layer on bottom of 9x13-inch pan.

SECOND LAYER
1 (8 ounce) package cream cheese, softened   1½ cups frozen whipped topping, thawed
1 cup powdered sugar

Mix cream cheese and powdered sugar. Add whipped topping. Layer on top of crust.

THIRD LAYER
1 (6 serving) package instant chocolate pudding.

Prepare pudding as directed. Layer on top of cream cheese mixture.

FOURTH LAYER
1 (8 ounce) carton frozen whipped topping,   Oreo cookie crumbs reserved from crust
thawed

Layer whipped topping on pudding and sprinkle with reserved crushed Oreo cookies. Chill.

Joanna Miller
Hersey, Michigan

Cherry O'Cream Cheese Pudding

CRUST
1½ cups graham cracker crumbs
¼ cup margarine, melted

¼ cup sugar

Mix graham cracker crumbs, margarine, and sugar. Press into 9x13-inch pan.

FILLING
1 (14 ounce) can sweetened condensed
  milk
1 (8 ounce) package cream cheese, softened
⅓ cup lemon juice

1 teaspoon vanilla
2 (20 ounce) cans cherry pie filling
1 (8 ounce) carton frozen whipped topping,
  thawed (optional)

Combine condensed milk and cream cheese. Add lemon juice and vanilla. Pour over graham cracker crust. Pour cherry pie filling over cream cheese mixture. Spread with whipped topping if desired. Chill.

Esther A. Hershberger
Goshen, Indiana

Food for Thought
It is better to look forward and prepare than to look back and despair.

Cinnamon Pudding

4 tablespoons margarine
4 cups packed brown sugar
4 cups water
2 cups flour
2 cups sugar
4 tablespoons margarine

4 teaspoons baking powder
4 teaspoons cinnamon
4 teaspoons vanilla
2¼ cups milk
¾ cup chopped nuts
Whipped topping or ice cream (optional)

Preheat oven to 350°. In saucepan, combine 4 tablespoons margarine, brown sugar, and water; bring to a boil. Meanwhile, combine flour, sugar, 4 tablespoons margarine, baking powder, cinnamon, vanilla, and milk; mix well. Spread in greased 9x13-inch pan and pour boiling sugar mixture over top. Bake 10 minutes. Sprinkle with nuts and bake 10 minutes longer. Serve warm with whipped topping or ice cream if desired.

Anna Stutzman
Arcola, Illinois

Some people, in order to discover God, read books.
But there is a great book: the very appearance of created things.
Look above you! Look below you! Read it.
Augustine

Caramel Pudding

1 stick (½ cup) margarine
2 cups packed brown sugar
Pinch soda
3 quarts milk

1 to 1½ cups ClearJel or 1 cup cornstarch
1 teaspoon vanilla
Pinch salt

....

Melt margarine and brown sugar in heavy saucepan, stirring constantly until browned. Stir in soda and milk. Heat until hot; then thicken with ClearJel. Add vanilla and salt. (For sweeter pudding, use less milk.)

Marion Stauffer
Mechanicsville, Maryland

Half the joy of life is in little things taken on the run. Let us run if we must—even the sands do that—but let us keep our hearts young and our eyes open that nothing worth our while shall escape us. And everything is worth its while if we only grasp it and its significance.

C. Victor Cherbuliez

Coffee Pudding

3 teaspoons instant coffee granules
½ cup warm water
1 (14 ounce) can sweetened condensed
  milk

1 (4 serving) package vanilla instant pudding
1½ cups water
1 cup frozen whipped topping, thawed

Dissolve coffee granules in warm water. Add condensed milk, pudding mix, water, and whipped topping; beat well. Let set before serving.

Janet M. Martin
Ephrata, Pennsylvania

Food for Thought
He who stands on his own strength will never stand.

Magic Mocha Pudding

1½ cups flour
1 cup sugar
2 teaspoons instant coffee granules
1 egg
2½ teaspoons baking powder
½ teaspoon salt
6 tablespoons butter
1 cup milk
Vanilla to taste

CHOCOLATE SAUCE

1 cup sugar
2 tablespoons cocoa
1½ tablespoons cornstarch
2½ cups water

Preheat oven to 350°. Combine pudding ingredients and mix well. Pour into baking dish. Combine sauce ingredients in saucepan and boil until thickened. Pour half of chocolate sauce over batter and bake 30 to 35 minutes. Add remaining sauce before serving. Serve hot with milk or cold with whipped cream.

Mrs. Gid Miller
Norwalk, Wisconsin

Raspberry Tapioca Pudding

1 (10 ounce) package frozen sweetened
    raspberries, thawed
1 cup purple grape juice
⅓ cup sugar

1 (1 inch) strip lemon peel
¼ cup instant tapioca
½ cup whipping cream
2 tablespoons powdered sugar

Mash and strain raspberries, reserving juice. Discard seeds. Add enough water to reserved raspberry juice to measure 2 cups. Pour into large saucepan; add grape juice, sugar, and lemon peel. Bring to a boil; reduce heat and simmer, uncovered, for 10 minutes. Remove lemon peel. Add tapioca and cook and stir for 10 minutes. Pour into custard cups. Cover and refrigerate for 4 hours or until set. In mixing bowl, beat whipping cream and powdered sugar until soft peaks form. Serve with pudding.

Edna Nisley
Baltic, Ohio

Prayer is as natural an expression of faith as breathing is of life.
Jonathan Edwards

Butterscotch Tapioca Pudding

6 cups boiling water
½ teaspoon salt
1½ cups pearl tapioca
2 cups packed brown sugar
2 eggs, beaten
½ cup sugar

1 cup milk
½ cup margarine, browned
1 teaspoon vanilla
2 to 3 bananas, sliced
1 (8 ounce) carton frozen whipped topping, thawed

In saucepan, combine water, salt, and tapioca; cook 15 minutes. Add brown sugar and cook until tapioca is clear. In small bowl, mix eggs, sugar, and milk; add to tapioca mixture. Cook until mixture bubbles. Add browned margarine and vanilla. Cool. To serve, spoon into custard cups and top with bananas and whipped topping.

Sarah Miller
Navarre, Ohio

Food for Thought

Every sunrise is a new message from God, and every sunset His signature.

Apple Tapioca Pudding

1 cup raisins
2 quarts water
½ cup instant tapioca
½ cup sugar

8 cups peeled and sliced apples
1 cup sugar (white or brown)
1 teaspoon cinnamon

Preheat oven to 375°. In saucepan, bring raisins and water to a boil. Combine tapioca and sugar; add to water, stirring constantly. Boil 3 to 5 minutes. Remove from heat. Mix sliced apples with sugar and cinnamon and spread in large greased baking or roasting pan. Pour tapioca mixture over apples. Bake 45 minutes or until apples are soft.

Mrs. Noah Shirk
Liberty, Kentucky

Rhubarb Pudding

4 cups diced rhubarb
1 cup water
¾ cup sugar
3 tablespoons instant tapioca

2 tablespoons margarine
2 teaspoons orange juice
⅓ teaspoon salt

Combine all ingredients in saucepan and let stand for 5 minutes. Heat to boiling and boil 1 minute. Reduce heat and simmer 5 minutes. Cool and serve.

Mary Miller
Heuvelton, New York

Rest is not idleness, and to lie sometimes on the grass under the trees on a summer's day, listening to the murmur of water, or watching the clouds float across the sky, is by no means a waste of time.

John Lubbock

Blackberry Pudding Cobbler

⅓ cup butter
2 cups sugar, divided
2 cups flour
1 teaspoon salt

2 teaspoons baking powder
1 cup milk
2 cups fresh or frozen blackberries
2 cups boiling water

....

Preheat oven to 350°. Cream butter and 1 cup sugar. Add flour, salt, baking powder, and milk to creamed mixture. Mix well and spread in greased 9x13-inch pan. Sprinkle blackberries on top of batter. Combine remaining 1 cup sugar and 2 cups boiling water and pour over berries. (May add more blackberries or liquid according to taste.) Bake 50 minutes. (Note: Other fruit or berries may be substituted for the blackberries.)

Mrs. Paul Schrock
Marion, Michigan

Food for Thought

Of all the things you wear, your expression is the most important.

Stove-Top Custard

2 cups milk
2 eggs, beaten
½ cup sugar (or less)

1 teaspoon vanilla
Dash salt
Dash nutmeg

Mix all ingredients just until blended. Pour into 4 custard cups (or coffee cups) and set cups in a kettle with an inch or two of cold water (kettle should have a tight-fitting lid). Bring to a boil, turn off heat, and let set for 45 minutes. Unbelievable, but this makes perfect custard.

Clara Yoder
Windsor, Missouri

Apple Walnut Cobbler

1¼ cups sugar, divided
½ teaspoon cinnamon
¾ cup coarsely chopped walnuts, divided
4 cups sliced tart apples
1 cup flour
1 teaspoon baking powder

¼ teaspoon salt
1 egg, well beaten
½ cup evaporated milk
⅓ cup margarine, melted
Whipped topping (optional)

Preheat oven to 325°. Mix ½ cup sugar, cinnamon, and ½ cup nuts. Spread apples in greased 8x8-inch baking dish. Sprinkle with cinnamon mixture. Sift remaining ¾ cup sugar, flour, baking powder, and salt. In large bowl, combine egg, evaporated milk, and margarine; add flour mixture and blend until smooth. Pour over apples. Sprinkle with remaining ¼ cup nuts. Bake 50 minutes. Serve with whipped topping or whipped cream sprinkled with cinnamon if desired.

Lois Rhodes
Harrisonburg, Virginia

Food for Thought

As a bright sunbeam comes into every window, so comes a love born of God's care for every need.

Magic Cobbler

½ cup butter
¾ cup milk
2 cups sugar, divided
1 cup flour

1½ teaspoons baking powder
2 cups fruit (peaches, apples, blueberries, blackberries, etc.)

Preheat oven to 350°. In 8x11-inch pan, melt butter. In mixing bowl, combine milk, 1 cup sugar, flour, and baking powder. Pour over melted butter but do not stir. Spread fruit on top and sprinkle with remaining 1 cup sugar. Again, do not stir. Bake 30 to 40 minutes or until fruit is soft.

Rosanna Helmuth
Arthur, Illinois

Your heart can rest in perfect security because God knows,
He loves, He leads.
A. B. Simpson

Blueberry Buckle

¾ cup sugar
¼ cup vegetable shortening
2 eggs
½ cup milk
1½ cups flour
2 teaspoons baking powder
¼ teaspoon nutmeg
Scant ¼ teaspoon cloves
½ teaspoon salt
1⅓ cups fresh blueberries

TOPPING
½ cup sugar
½ cup chopped nuts
⅓ cup flour
½ teaspoon cinnamon
¼ cup butter

Preheat oven to 375°. Mix sugar, shortening, eggs, and milk. Stir in flour, baking powder, nutmeg, cloves, and salt. Fold in blueberries and spread into greased 9x9-inch pan. Mix topping ingredients and sprinkle over batter. Bake 45 to 50 minutes. Serve warm with milk.

Mrs. Gid Miller
Norwalk, Wisconsin

Other Desserts

And also that every man should eat and drink,
and enjoy the good of all his labour, it is the gift of God.

ECCLESIASTES 3:13

Simple Caramel Krispy Rolls

2 cups packed brown sugar
1 (14 ounce) can sweetened condensed
  milk
1 cup light corn syrup
1½ cups butter, divided
8 cups miniature marshmallows
10 cups crisp rice cereal

....

In saucepan, combine brown sugar, condensed milk, corn syrup, and 1 cup butter. Boil 12 minutes, stirring constantly. Cool. Meanwhile, melt remaining ½ cup butter over low heat. Add marshmallows and melt, stirring constantly. Add crisp rice cereal and mix well. Spread to ½ inch thick on large buttered baking sheets. Spread cooled caramel mixture on top, roll up jelly roll style, and slice.

Saloma Stutzman
Navarre, Ohio

The sun. . .in its full glory, either at rising or setting—
this, and many other like blessings, we enjoy daily;
and for the most of them, because they are so common,
most men forget to pay their praises. But let not us.
Izaak Walton

Broken Glass Dessert

24 graham crackers, crushed
½ cup packed brown sugar
¼ cup butter, melted
3 (3 ounce) packages gelatin (assorted flavors)

2 cups frozen whipped topping, thawed
1 (8 ounce) package cream cheese, softened
½ cup sugar
1 teaspoon vanilla
1 cup crushed pineapple, drained

Mix graham cracker crumbs, brown sugar, and butter. Reserve ¼ cup crumbs and press remaining crumbs into glass 9x13-inch pan or large bowl. Dissolve each package of flavored gelatin in ½ cup boiling water. Chill gelatin in separate pans. Cut into cubes. Beat whipped topping, cream cheese, sugar, and vanilla. Fold in pineapple and gelatin cubes. Spread on top of crumb crust. Sprinkle with reserved crumbs. Chill.

Maria Schrock
Princeton, Missouri

Granny Smith Apple Dessert

1 Granny Smith apple
1 tube crescent rolls
1 stick (½ cup) butter

1 cup packed brown sugar
1 cup Mountain Dew

Preheat oven to 350°. Peel and core apple. Cut into 8 slices. Microwave slices 2 minutes on paper towel or bake in 250° oven 5 to 6 minutes. Wrap each apple slice in a crescent roll and place in 8x8-inch pan. Melt butter and brown sugar. Do not boil. Pour over rolls. Then pour Mountain Dew over mixture. Bake 50 minutes or until golden brown and set.

Ida Marchand
Goshen, Indiana

Pineapple Rings

1 can (14 ounce) sweetened condensed
  milk
1 can pineapple slices (10 slices)

Frozen whipped topping, thawed
Maraschino cherries (optional)

Cook unopened can of condensed milk for 3 hours in kettle of water. Make sure water covers can at all times. Then refrigerate can until cold. Spread out pineapple slices on a plate. Open both ends of milk can with can opener. Remove one end and use the other to push up thickened milk. Cut milk into 10 slices as you push up from bottom. (To make cutting easier, dip knife blade in boiling water between every cut.) Top each pineapple slice with a milk slice. Then top each with a dab of whipped topping and garnish with a maraschino cherry if desired.

Dianna Yoder
Goshen, Indiana

Be on the lookout for mercies.
The more we look for them, the more of them we will see.
Blessings brighten when we count them.
Maltbie D. Babcock

Blueberry Cream Cheese Squares

¼ cup cornstarch
½ cup sugar
½ cup water
⅓ cup blueberries (drained)
2 cups graham cracker crumbs
1½ sticks (¾ cup) butter, melted

1½ cups sugar
2 teaspoons vanilla
2 (8 ounce) packages cream cheese,
  softened
1 package Dream Whip or ¾ cup cream,
  whipped

Combine cornstarch, sugar, water, and blueberries. Cook until thick. Cool. Combine graham cracker crumbs and melted butter. Press two-thirds of crumbs into 9x13-inch pan, reserving remaining crumbs for top. Beat sugar and vanilla into cream cheese. Fold in whipped topping. Spread half of cream cheese mixture over crumbs. Spread blueberry filling over cheese layer. Layer remaining cheese mixture over blueberries and top with reserved crumbs. Chill. (Note: Raspberries or cherries may be substituted for the blueberries.)

Ida C. Miller
Medford, Wisconsin

Food for Thought

Wisdom has two parts: having much to say and not saying much at all.

Strawberry Pizza

½ cup margarine
1¼ cups sugar, divided
1 egg
1⅓ cups flour
¼ teaspoon salt
1 teaspoon baking powder

1 (8 ounce) package cream cheese, softened
1 (8 ounce) carton frozen whipped topping, thawed
1½ quarts strawberries
1 package strawberry glaze

Preheat oven to 375°. Cream margarine, ¾ cup sugar, and egg. Add flour, salt, and baking powder. Spread on pizza pan and bake 10 minutes. Combine cream cheese, remaining ½ cup sugar, and whipped topping. Spread over cooled crust. Combine strawberries and glaze; spread over top. Refrigerate to set.

Mrs. Paul H. Schwartz Sr.
Fremont, Michigan

Food for Thought

Prayer is not a way of getting what we want, but the way to become what God wants us to be.

Cottage Cheese Dessert

1 (3 ounce) package gelatin (any flavor)
1 (8 ounce) can crushed pineapple,
   drained (juice reserved)

1 (12 ounce) carton cottage cheese
1 (12 ounce) carton frozen whipped
   topping, thawed

....

Stir dry gelatin into pineapple juice. Mix cottage cheese and whipped topping. Add pineapple and gelatin mixture. Chill.

Mrs. Norman L. Miller
Clark, Missouri

The Lord gives you the experience of enjoying His presence. He touches you, and His touch is so delightful that, more than ever, you are drawn inwardly to Him.
Madame Jeanne Guyon

Scotcharoos

1 cup sugar	6 cups crisp rice cereal
1 cup light corn syrup	1 cup chocolate chips
1 cup peanut butter	1 cup butterscotch chips

In large saucepan, mix sugar and corn syrup. Bring just to a boil. Remove from heat and add peanut butter and crisp rice cereal. Mix thoroughly. Press into greased 9x13-inch pan. In double boiler, melt chocolate and butterscotch chips and spread over crisp rice cereal.

Linda Stoltzfus
Orrstown, Pennsylvania

Food for Thought

The highest reward for our toil is not what we get for it but what we become by it.

Apple Goodie

5 to 6 apples, peeled and sliced
¾ teaspoon cinnamon
½ cup sugar
1 cup quick oats

¾ cup packed brown sugar
½ cup flour
⅛ teaspoon salt
⅓ cup butter

Preheat oven to 350°. Spread apples in 9x9-inch baking dish. Sprinkle with mixture of cinnamon and sugar. Mix oats, brown sugar, flour, salt, and butter until crumbly; sprinkle on top of apples. Bake 35 minutes or until apples are soft. Serve warm with milk or ice cream.

Sarah Schwartz
Marlette, Michigan

Food for Thought

When we are willing to do what we can, we will be surprised at how much we can do.

Rhubarb Dessert

4 cups diced rhubarb
1 cup sugar
1 (3 ounce) package strawberry gelatin

1 cake mix (white or yellow)
2 cups water

Preheat oven to 350°. Layer ingredients in order given in 9x13-inch pan. Do not stir. Bake 40 minutes.

Janet Martin
Ephrata, Pennsylvania

Let your strivings, then, be after contentment.
Get out of each passing day all the sweetness there is in it.
Live in the present hour as much as possible,
and if you live for character, your foundations
will outlast tomorrow.
George H. Hepworth

Pumpkin Rolls

3 eggs
1 cup sugar
⅔ cup pumpkin
1 teaspoon lemon juice
¾ cup flour
1 teaspoon baking powder
2 teaspoons cinnamon
1 teaspoon ginger
½ teaspoon nutmeg
½ teaspoon salt

FILLING
1 cup powdered sugar
¼ cup butter, softened
6 ounces cream cheese
1 teaspoon vanilla

Preheat oven to 375°. Beat eggs on high speed for 5 minutes. Beat in sugar. Stir in pumpkin and lemon juice. Combine dry ingredients and fold into pumpkin mixture. Spread into greased and floured 10x15-inch pan. Bake 15 minutes. Remove cake from oven and turn onto clean linen towel dusted with powdered sugar. Roll towel and cake together. Cool. Blend filling ingredients until smooth. Unroll cooled cake; spread with filling and roll back up.

Elizabeth Borntrager
Brown City, Michigan

Rhubarb Torte

CRUST
1½ cups flour

2 tablespoons sugar

Pinch salt

½ cup butter

Preheat oven to 325°. Mix crust ingredients until crumbly and press into 8x10-inch pan. Bake 20 to 25 minutes.

FILLING
2¼ cups diced rhubarb

1½ cups sugar

2 to 3 cups whole milk

2 to 4 tablespoons flour

3 egg yolks

1 teaspoon vanilla

Combine filling ingredients in saucepan and cook until thick. Pour over crust.

TOPPING
3 egg whites

¼ teaspoon cream of tartar

6 tablespoons sugar

Preheat oven to 350°. Beat topping ingredients until stiff. Spread over filling. Bake 10 to 15 minutes or until lightly browned.

Mrs. Bruce Troyer
Crab Orchard, Kentucky

Apple Pandowdy

FILLING

4 cups peeled and sliced apples
1 cup packed brown sugar
¼ cup flour
½ teaspoon salt

1 tablespoon vinegar
¾ cup water
1 tablespoon butter
1 teaspoon vanilla

Preheat oven to 400°. Spread apples in 9x13-inch pan. To make syrup, combine brown sugar, flour, salt, vinegar, and water in saucepan. Bring to a boil and cook 2 minutes. Remove from heat and add butter and vanilla. Pour over apples.

TOPPING

1 cup flour
½ teaspoon salt
2 teaspoons baking powder

2½ tablespoons shortening
½ cup milk

Mix flour, salt, baking powder, and shortening with pastry cutter. Add milk and stir just until moistened. Drop by spoonfuls over apple filling. Bake 35 minutes. Serve with whole milk or cream.

Marie Zimmerman
Pembroke, Kentucky

Banana Split Dessert

3 cups graham cracker crumbs
½ cup margarine, melted
1 (8 ounce) package cream cheese, softened
1½ cups powdered sugar
1 teaspoon vanilla
1 (20 ounce) can crushed pineapple, drained

3 bananas, sliced
1 (16 ounce) carton frozen whipped topping, thawed
Chocolate syrup

Preheat oven to 350°. Combine graham cracker crumbs and melted margarine. Press into 9x13-inch pan and bake 5 minutes. Cool. Mix cream cheese, powdered sugar, and vanilla. Spread over crust. Spread pineapple on top of cream cheese; arrange bananas on top of pineapple. Top with whipped topping and drizzle with chocolate syrup. Refrigerate.

Carolyn Wenger
Elk Horn, Kentucky

Blueberry Dessert

1½ cups graham cracker crumbs
½ cup butter or margarine, melted
1 (8 ounce) package cream cheese, softened
2 eggs

1 cup sugar
1 (21 ounce) can blueberry pie filling
Whipped topping (optional)

Preheat oven to 350°. Combine graham cracker crumbs and melted butter. Press into 8x11-inch glass baking dish. Mix cream cheese, eggs, and sugar until smooth and pour over crumb crust. Bake 20 minutes or until brown around edges. Cool. Spread pie filling over cream cheese layer. Top with whipped topping if desired.

Mrs. Paul Schrock
Marion, Michigan

Food for Thought
People can't stumble when they are on their knees.

Raisin Mumbles

FILLING
2½ cups raisins
½ cup sugar
2 tablespoons cornstarch
1 cup water
3 tablespoons lemon juice

CRUMB MIXTURE
¼ cup butter
1 cup packed brown sugar
½ teaspoon baking soda
1½ cups quick oats
Scant 1¾ cups flour

Preheat oven to 350°. Cook filling ingredients in saucepan over low heat, stirring constantly until thick (about 5 minutes). Cool. Meanwhile, cream butter and brown sugar. Add soda, oats, and flour; mix well. Press half of crumb mixture into 9x13-inch pan. Spread filling on top; sprinkle with remaining crumbs. Bake 25 to 30 minutes.

Lydia Hoover
Denver, Pennsylvania

In our daily practice of prayer, we should begin each day with an act of loving thankfulness to God.
C. F. Andrews

Index